Rock-a-Bye Baby

Rock-a-Bye Baby

200 WAYS TO HELP BABY (AND YOU!)
SLEEP BETTER

By Penny Warner
With a Foreword by Louis Borgenicht, M.D.

Illustrations by Ashley Alexander

CHRONICLE BOOKS
SAN FRANCISCO

Library of Congress Cataloging-in-Publication Data:
Warner, Penny.
  Rock-a-bye baby : 200 ways to help baby (and you!) sleep better /
by Penny Warner ; with a foreword by Louis Borgenicht.
    p. cm.
  Includes index.
  ISBN: 978-0-8118-6149-6
  1. Infants--Care. 2. Infants--Sleep. 3. Parent and infant. 4. Child rearing.
  I. Title.
  HQ774.W365 2008
  649'.122--dc22

                              2007033943

Printed in China
Designed by Jennifer Tolo Pierce
10 9 8 7 6 5 4 3 2 1

Chronicle Books LLC
680 Second Street
San Francisco, California 94107
www.chroniclebooks.com

To Bradley

A joy when awake, a cherub when asleep.

To Luke

Who's just beginning to wake up.

Table of Contents

Foreword

Changes in child care occur with ever-increasing speed these days. As a pediatrician, I've tracked the trends in medical journals and among my colleagues and patients for more than thirty years. The constant renewal is a clear mirror for our cultural need to always get the newest, best, and most accurate information—which is a tough pace to jog at when you're having your first child.

In stark contrast to this frenzy stands parental intuition, a constant and powerful force in child-rearing that, in the face of information overload, needs constant reinforcement. Dr. Spock's paean to parents to "Trust yourself. You know more than you think you do," still resonates prominently today. In fact, it's never been truer. No wonder his 1946 book, *Baby and Child Care,* has long been considered the bible of child care and remains a best-seller more than sixty years later.

But not all child-care advice is as evergreen. More than eighty years ago, L. Emmett Holt, M.D., published *The Care and Feeding of Children: A Catechism for the Use of Mothers and Children's Nurses*. It was designed to make simple and very concrete sense of parental concerns. The book contains questions and answers (both concocted by Holt), usually leaving little room for variance.

On the matter of sleep, he commented:

Q: Should a child sleep in the same bed as his mother or nurse?

    A: Never, if this can be possibly avoided.

Q: Is rocking necessary?

    A: By no means. It is a habit easily acquired, but hard to break, and a very useless and injurious one.

Holt's catechism seems formulaic in a world in which flexibility is *de rigueur*. Then, and perhaps even more now, rigidity causes a world of worry for parents. Because there is no *one way* to give your child a safe and healthy upbringing; accepting this notion may make parenting in the twenty-first century easier.

With so many experts opining different truths, attitudes toward and anxiety about infant sleeping begin even before a baby is born. Actual and apocryphal tales of somnolent terror color the perspective of virtually every new parent. To ease the worry, pediatricians now often speak with prospective parents well before the child is born—here's that need for the best information again. When I meet with an expectant couple, I emphasize two things that seem to be helpful: the confusion of the first two weeks post-pregnancy, and parental guilt. Both themes are designed to help parents deal comfortably with their new roles.

My talk goes something like this: The first two weeks of life with your new baby will be unlike any others in your life. Your relationship with each other changes as you try to understand your baby and figure out how to care for her. Despite what you may have been told by friends and relatives and what you may have read, you actually know a lot more about taking care of your child than you think you do. This will be a process of trusting yourself, most likely with the assistance of a few judicious questions for your pediatrician.

During those first two weeks and for the years following, remember that once you decided to become parents, you bought into guilt. I've noticed that parents feel they can maintain control over their children's lives by dredging up their guilt as an explanation for the adversity their children encounter. For example, a parent may believe that his child's cold is due to neglect—for example, not having dressed his child warmly enough. But I promise you, not everything is your fault. Having some perspective on the convoluted paths of parental guilt may make it less daunting.

All this aside, there is no one simple answer to sleep issues. This book offers more than 200 answers, some of which will ultimately apply to your family if you believe in yourself and your own ability to understand your child.

Remember: your relationship with your child, whether awake or asleep, is an ever-changing process, and your intuition is your most helpful asset.

—Louis Borgenicht, M.D.

Introduction

Nothing brings a smile to a mother or father's face faster than the cherubic look of their sleeping baby. And nothing brings on the tears like an overtired, not-so-cherubic child who can't, or won't, go to sleep.

I should know. I spent the first couple of years of my babies' lives in a twilight daze brought on by lack of sleep—theirs and mine. Even with a couple of academic degrees in child development, I didn't have a clue how to get my little angels off to snoozeville; that elusive secret simply wasn't covered in the clinical textbooks I had studied.

It wasn't until I began teaching parenting classes that I learned the sleep secrets held only by the real experts: experienced parents. I started collecting the tips they shared, knowing there were a lot of droopy-eyed parents out there searching for help. When it came time to write this book, I had more than 200 parent-approved suggestions! How could I not share these wonderful tips with other night-zombie parents when I had them at my fingertips?

Whether you're expecting your first child (congratulations!) or enjoying the birth of your second, third, or tenth (goodness!), sleep can feel like a big challenge, for both you and your child. But it doesn't have to be. With these tried-and-true (and even a little wacky) tips, sleep can be all it's supposed to be: hours upon hours of restful bliss. Sound like a dream? *Rock-a-Bye Baby* makes it a reality.

You'll find in this book everything from parents' and grandparents' time-tested wisdom to recommendations from credentialed pediatricians and child-development specialists. There's certainly no shortage of advice. The trick is to make your way through it all, try many different pointers, and find the few that suit your and your baby's lifestyle and routine. Because, trust me, everyone has an opinion about what works best! It's the rare parent who doesn't get an earful of sleep tips from well-meaning family and friends, not to mention the glut of parenting magazines, blogs, and online support groups. Here you'll find all the tips you'll need from a variety of sources, conveniently gathered in one place so you're never stuck searching for an answer in moments of exhaustion.

Sure, the sleep issue can be overwhelming, but there's no reason to despair. Trust your instincts about which of these suggestions are best for you and your baby. Because while doctors are certainly trustworthy sources—they're experts for a reason, and their advice is worth a try—perhaps no one has more expertise than parents, who have earned their MOM. or DAD.

degree as late-night sleep consultants. They've walked a mile in your slippers and tend to have the most helpful, practical advice.

When you need a hand, dip into this book. The tips are arranged by theme so you can search for targeted advice. They're also short and sweet, so you can flip to a random page for instant suggestions at frantic moments. It's like having your own personal baby nurse—minus the exorbitant price tag, of course. Many tips may be new to you—bouncing on the exercise ball, climbing up and down stairs, wrapping up a ticking clock—and some will be familiar—rocking your baby in a sling, taking him for a ride in the car, singing her a lullaby— but each one is worth trying. You never know what will work this time, so don't rule out anything.

And remember: Not all babies, and not all parents, are the same. So despite all the knowing advice in this book, paying attention to your baby's moods and temperament is the best way to learn her sleeping patterns. Understanding these patterns will help you get to the bottom of why she might not be falling asleep easily. While some babies are more wakeful and others sleepier, most newborns sleep sixteen hours a day—in three-to-four-hour periods, that is. (Can you imagine your baby sleeping sixteen hours straight? Talk about sweet dreams.) The good news is by three months of age, 70 percent of babies sleep from midnight to 5 A.M. But that means that 30 percent do not. And that's perfectly normal—sleep problems are typical in the first year or two of your child's life. After that, 85 percent of children go to sleep peacefully—after that last drink of water, that last bedtime story, and that last goodnight kiss, of course.

Also, you're not alone. This book, not to mention the support of your family, friends, and doctors, will help make the process quick, easy, and effective for your baby. As a matter of fact, this is a great resource to keep cribside for your babysitter, nanny, or parents to use at bedtime. Just flag your favorite techniques and leave with confidence that everyone will rest easy.

At the end of the day, sleep does not have to be a mystery. I'm certain you'll discover the answer to the age-old question: How do I get my baby to sleep? You'll find the Sandman is there before you know it. I should know. Many of these tips worked for me and they worked for all the parents and other experts who contributed to this book. We've got the bright eyes and restful smiles to prove it!

A Few Important Caveats

To be sure your baby is safe and healthy, always follow this medical advice from the American Academy of Pediatrics and the National Safety Council before trying a particular method for getting your baby to sleep.

Check with Doc

The first thing to do is discuss your baby's sleep problems with your pediatrician, so you can rule out any medical or physical reasons for poor sleep.

Back to Sleep

Always put your baby on his back to sleep, to help prevent Sudden Infant Death Syndrome (SIDS). Studies have shown that having babies sleep on their backs cuts their risk of SIDS in half.

SUDDEN INFANT DEATH SYNDROME—WHAT YOU NEED TO KNOW

Sudden Infant Death Syndrome, also known as SIDS, is one of the most frightening concerns of parents with infants. A lot of research has been done, and continues today, on the syndrome. While we don't yet have all the answers, some promising discoveries have been made, and there are a few ways you can help prevent SIDS from occurring. Here's the latest information.

- SIDS is defined as "the sudden death of an infant under one year of age that remains unexplained after thorough case investigation."

- Researchers believe that babies who die of SIDS have one or more innate conditions that make them vulnerable.

- SIDS occurs in all types of families, regardless of race or socioeconomic level, and is the leading cause of death in infants.

- SIDS usually occurs between one month and one year of age, with the highest risk between two and four months.

- SIDS is sudden, silent, and associated with sleep, with no signs of suffering involved. It is not caused by vomiting, choking, minor illnesses, vaccines, or child abuse.

- Risk factors that apply to the mother of the child include cigarette smoking during pregnancy, maternal age less than twenty years, poor prenatal care, low weight gain, anemia, use of illegal drugs before

or during pregnancy and breast-feeding, and history
of sexually transmitted diseases.

*While you cannot eliminate the risk of SIDS entirely, you can lower
the risk by:*

- Having your baby sleep on her back. (Turn her head
  to the side to prevent it from becoming flat, known
  as flathead syndrome.)

- Using a firm mattress without excess padding or
  loose bedding.

- Not putting more than one or two soft toys in the crib.

- Not sleeping with baby (to prevent rolling over on her),
  but having her sleep in her own crib in your room.

- Encouraging baby to use a pacifier.

- Not smoking during pregnancy (and not having
  secondhand smoke around baby).

- Not overheating the baby or the room.

- Not relying solely on monitors for safety.

- Encouraging "tummy time" when your baby is awake,
  to enhance motor development and respiration.

- Not letting your baby spend too much time in carriers
  or bouncers.

Warm, Not Hot

Don't overheat your baby in an effort to keep her warm.
Maintain the temperature of the room between 65° and 72° F.
Avoid putting your baby by the window, to keep her from
bursts of cold air or direct sunlight.

Blanket Policy

Don't overdo it with blankets, comforters, and sheets, or your baby
might get tangled up or overheated during the night. Dress him in
a flame-resistant, loose-fitting sleeper if it's chilly.

No Pillow Talk

Babies don't need pillows, and they can dangerously restrict their
breathing. If you think your baby will sleep better if her head is
inclined, you can buy a wedge that will gently lift your baby's head
without endangering her breathing.

Just Right

Make sure your baby's mattress isn't too soft or too hard. Try it out yourself by laying it on the floor and stretching out on it; if you are uncomfortable, your baby may be, too. A mattress that's too hard has no give, and a mattress that's too soft offers little support.

⟶ ⟫ ● ⟪ ⟵

Soft and Snuggly

Let your baby sleep with a special "lovey," such as a soft blanket, stuffed animal, or treasured toy—but make sure the blanket isn't too thick and the stuffed animal isn't too big, so they won't inhibit his breathing if he gets too close to them.

⟶ ⟫ ● ⟪ ⟵

Plenty of Pacifiers

Offer your baby a pacifier to help her sleep (and help prevent SIDS), but never tie it or anything else to your baby's clothing, because it could get tangled around her neck and cause strangulation. Just sprinkle several pacifiers in the crib, so she has easy access to another if one is lost.

———— ✐ ⊃ ● ⊂ ✐ ————

Keep Watch

Never leave your baby sleeping unattended in the stroller, swing, or car seat.

———— ✐ ⊃ ● ⊂ ✐ ————

Watch Dogs . . . and Cats

Don't allow Spot or Fluffy access to your sleeping baby. In fact, don't ever leave your baby—even when awake—unattended with a pet.

———— ✐ ⊃ ● ⊂ ✐ ————

CRIB-SAFETY TIPS

Here are some tips for crib safety from the National Safety Council.

CRIB DESIGN

- If your crib was built before 1974, make sure the slats are no more than 2 $\frac{3}{8}$ inches apart—otherwise, your infant may get his head stuck between them.

- Corner posts should be the same height as, or less than $\frac{1}{16}$ inch higher than, the end panels, to prevent your baby from catching a part of her clothing on one and strangling.

- There shouldn't be any sharp edges or carvings on the headboard or footboard.

- In their raised position, the top rails of the crib sides should be at least 26 inches above the top of the mattress support at its lowest position, so Baby cannot climb out and fall.

MATTRESS

- The mattress should fit snugly in the crib without any gaps, so your baby can't become trapped.

- Don't use any plastic materials, such as plastic sheets, in or near the crib.

- Put your baby to sleep on his back in a crib with a firm, flat mattress and no soft bedding underneath, to prevent SIDS and suffocation.

(continued)

CRIB HARDWARE

- It should require two distinct actions, or a minimum force of 10 pounds with one action, to release the latch or the locks on the drop side(s) of the crib, so your child cannot accidentally release it.

- Make sure none of the hardware is disengaged, broken, bent, or loose. Also check that the mattress support hangers and brackets are secure and cannot drop. The hardware and the crib should be smooth and free of sharp edges, points, and rough surfaces.

CRIB ACCESSORIES

- Be cautious with bumper pads. They should cover the entire inside perimeter of the crib and tie or snap securely in place. And they should have at least six straps or ties (cut off any excess).

- Check the teething rails. If they are damaged, fix, replace, or remove them immediately.

- To prevent possible entanglement, mobiles and crib gyms, which are meant to be hung over or across the crib, should be removed when your child is five months old, or first able to stand or climb.

- Keep the crib clear of plastic sheets, pillows, and large stuffed animals or toys, which can be suffocation hazards and can also enable your child to climb out of the crib.

CRIB ENVIRONMENT
- Do not place the crib by the window. Drapes and blind cords are dangerous—children can get caught in them. Also, there's the risk of falling out the window as your baby becomes able to climb up and stand.

- Install a smoke detector in your baby's room, following the manufacturer's directions for placement.

Crib Notes

Make sure your crib meets safety requirements:
The mattress should fit snugly with no gaps, and the sheets
should be snug and secure.

Baby Monitor

Use a baby monitor to listen for your baby while he
is sleeping. Or install a video camera, if you want to keep
an eye on your sleeping baby.

Co-sleeping Concerns

Seventy percent of parents co-sleep with Baby at one time
or another. But make sure that your bed is a safe sleeping
environment for your baby and that she can't roll off, and that
there's plenty of room for all. If you're a deep sleeper, drink
alcohol, or take drugs, you risk rolling over on your baby,
so co-sleeping is not recommended. And if you snore,
you may keep your baby awake!

BEDTIME DOS AND DON'TS

Here are some simple dos and don'ts to keep in mind when it's time for bed.

- - Don't put your baby on her tummy to sleep.

- + Do put her on her back to sleep.

- - Don't give your baby any alcohol or adult medications to get her to sleep.

- + Do check with your doctor to see if a baby medication, such as Infants' Tylenol, might help.

- - Don't let your baby go to sleep with a bottle of juice or milk, which may lead to tooth decay.

- + Do let your baby have a pacifier or a bottle of water if she wants it.

- - Don't give your baby herbal teas, except those approved by your pediatrician.

- + Do give her watered down juice if she doesn't like plain water.

- - Don't ever shake, vigorously tickle, or roughhouse with your baby.

- + Do play with her gently—games such as peekaboo or patty-cake.

Chapter 1

Expert Advice

○) ● (○

"Sleep 'til you're hungry, eat 'til you're sleepy."
—*author unknown*

Begin your quest for your baby's sleep solution by discussing your concerns with your baby's doctor. She will check to see if there are any medical reasons causing the problem and, if so, begin treatment. Once medical issues have been ruled out, you can move on to find a tip or method that works for you. Here are some general suggestions I gathered from the American Academy of Pediatrics, the National Safety Council, La Leche League, professional sleep consultants, and child developmentalists to get you started. Their medically researched recommendations are basics you can trust, and you'll always be glad you have them at the ready.

TYPICAL SLEEP PATTERNS FOR BABIES

Although it may not seem like it, newborns sleep about sixteen hours a day, but only for three to four hours at a time. Here's what you can expect:

- Seventy percent of babies sleep from midnight to 5 A.M. by three months.

- Eighty-five percent sleep through the night by six months.

- A stretch of five hours is considered "sleeping through the night."

- Babies have tiny tummies, so they wake up often for the next feeding. Breast milk is easily—and therefore quickly—digested.

Breast-feed Baby

There's evidence that breast milk contains serotonins, which naturally relax Baby and help get him to sleep, so simply breast-feeding may help him doze off.

Stay on Schedule

Put your baby on a regular schedule for naps and bedtime,
so her body is trained to anticipate sleep on cue.

Doses After Shots

Babies are sometimes fussy after their immunizations.
With your doctor's permission, you can give her a minimal dose
of Infants' Tylenol.

Rash Judgment

An irritated bottom can keep your baby from sleeping.
At the first sign of diaper rash (redness), use a medication
like Desenex to clear it up.

Keep an Eye Out

Watch for signs your baby is tired—such as yawning,
rubbing eyes, whining, or getting cranky—and then put your baby
to bed before he becomes overtired.

SEVEN SIGNS OF (HURRAH!) SLEEPINESS

So baby doesn't want to go to sleep—but is she betraying her own exhaustion? Check for these telltale signs of sleepiness before pushing for a nap.

1. Rubbing eyes

2. Yawning

3. Fussing, whining

4. Lying down

5. Slowing down

6. Slow blinking

7. Glazed look

NOTE: These can also be signs of illness, so check with your doctor if you have any concerns.

Skip the Nap

While parents are often reluctant to give up on Baby's nap, some babies just don't need the extra sleep anymore. Omitting an unnecessary nap may help Baby sleep better at night.

On the Other Hand

Some babies sleep better at night if they have a good nap in
the daytime. And if they miss it, they may be overtired and have
trouble sleeping during the night.

Set the Stage

Make sure the room is conducive to sleep, with closed blinds,
a comfy crib, cozy "loveys," and a quiet atmosphere. This helps
your baby know it's nap time.

Hold Off Responding

Unless your baby is crying hysterically, don't respond every time
she calls out. She may learn to go to sleep on her own.

Wrap Baby Up

Swaddling your baby—wrapping him snugly in a swaddling
blanket or a swaddler—makes him feel more secure, which can
calm down a fussy baby. Swaddling also keeps your baby warm
and prevents him from startling awake.

SAFE SWADDLING

Swaddling can be magical. By wrapping your baby up in a cozy blanket so she can't flail her arms and legs or startle herself, you'll make her feel more secure, as if she's all cuddled up in the womb. And swaddling isn't just great for encouraging sleep and relaxation—it also comforts babies who are upset, scared, or overly tired. Here's a simple way to swaddle your baby. Just be sure to chat and reassure her as you do.

1. Choose a lightweight cotton blanket with some give or stretch.

2. Lay the blanket on the floor at an angle.

3. Fold down the top corner about a quarter of the way.

4. Place your baby on the blanket, head above the fold.

5. Fold your baby's arms over her chest—don't leave them straight at the sides. Remember, you want to wrap your baby's arms within the blanket so she can't flail them.

6. Wrap one corner of the blanket over her arms and chest, and tuck it into the side of baby and blanket.

7. Bring the bottom corner up, allowing a little room for Baby's legs to move, and fold and tuck it into the top of the blanket.

8. Wrap the other corner around baby, and tuck it around Baby's back.

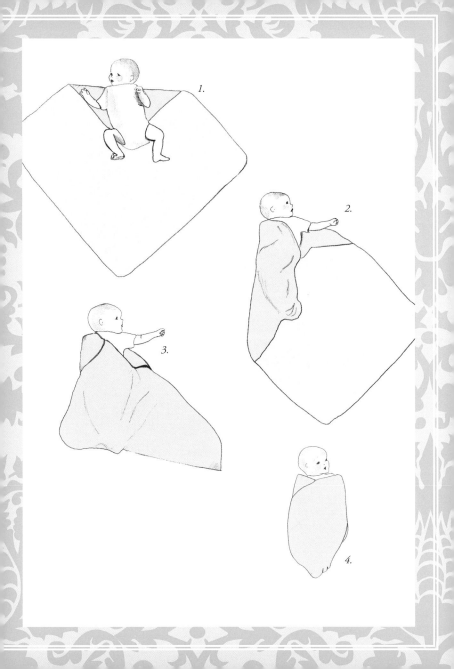

1.

2.

3.

4.

Got Good Milk?

Avoid alcohol and caffeinated drinks if you're breast-feeding.
These drinks go through your breast milk and not only affect
your baby, but they may also cause restless sleep.

Suck to Sleep

Some babies refuse to take a pacifier, but others seem
to need one to sleep. Let your baby suck her thumb or
a pacifier to help soothe her.

Check Current Conditions

Make sure your baby's room is comfortable—not too cool,
not too warm—when the door is open or closed.

Rise and Shine

Gently rouse your baby in the morning if he sleeps late. Your
baby's body clock may be off, so waking him earlier may encourage
better, not longer, sleep.

The Right Bed

Buy a comfortable bed for your baby, with a soft
but firm and supportive mattress pad. If you line the mattress
with plastic to keep it dry, make sure you add an extra pad
over the lining for comfort.

Active Play

When your baby is awake during the day, spend some time
playing together to help burn up energy, so she will sleep better
at night. Try a game of peekaboo, bicycle legs (rotating baby's legs
as if she's peddling a bicycle), or "I'm gonna get you!"

Create a Routine

Perform the same ritual each time you put your baby down
for a nap. For example, give your baby a bath, sing a song,
rock your baby, and then put him down. Soon he will associate
this pattern with sleep—and when you start the first steps,
he will already be ready for what lies ahead.

Downtime

Give your baby a chance to wind down by stopping
vigorous activity fifteen to twenty minutes before you want her
to fall asleep. Switch to quiet activities, such as singing to,
bathing, or rocking her.

Let It Be

Some babies wake up in the night, wiggle and squirm and
make noise, then miraculously return to sleep. So don't react too
quickly—give your baby a chance to settle down on his own.

Keep It Calm

When your baby awakens in the middle of the night for
a feeding, keep the lights dim, and use a soft voice and slow
movements, so your baby will not be roused during nursing.

Baby Knows Best

Sometimes you just need to adjust your routine to fit your
baby's needs, simply to make life easier for everyone.

WHY DO BABIES WAKE UP AT NIGHT?

The most common reasons are:

- Hunger, especially during growth spurts

- Teething, usually accompanied by a lot of drooling

- Developmental steps, such as crawling, walking, etc., which may cause changes in their sleep due to excessive energy or tiredness

- Illness, such as a cold or flu, that causes congestion

- Discomfort due to allergy, diaper rash, or eczema

- Loneliness—baby wants to be with Mom or Dad

- Reversal of day and night cycles—baby is used to sleeping in the womb while being rocked during the daytime and waking up while Mom's asleep at night

- Being startled by a dream, a noise, or a sudden twitch

- Extreme temperature—the room is too warm or too cool

HOW DO THE EXPERTS COMPARE?

Here's a short list of the leading sleep experts and their varying approaches.

EXPERT	APPROACH
American Academy of Pediatrics	Teach baby to go to sleep on his own. Help baby distinguish night from day. Wake baby from naps so he will sleep longer at night.
T. Berry Brazelton, M.D., author of *Sleep: The Brazelton Way*	Don't let Baby cry it out—instead, let her comfort herself for a few minutes before you respond and she may return to sleep. If Baby is upset, pat and reassure her, then leave, returning as necessary. Develop bedtime rituals.
Richard Ferber, M.D., author of *Solve Your Baby's Sleep Problems*	Form good sleep patterns by allowing Baby to cry himself to sleep alone.

EXPERT	APPROACH
Jodi A. Mindell, M.D., author of *Sleeping Through the Night*	Establish good sleep habits by having a consistent sleep time. Put your baby down when she's still awake. Replace "negative sleep associations" with positive ones.
William Sears, M.D., author of *The Baby Sleep Book*	Be there to provide comfort to Baby in a relaxing environment, and sleep will come naturally. Baby will learn that bedtime and sleep are pleasant experiences.

Chapter 2

Golden Standards
That Still Work

○) ● (○

"People who say they sleep like babies usually don't have them."
—Leo J. Burke

I n this chapter you'll find the most popular ways to get baby to sleep, passed on from parent to parent over the years. Although not all babies are the same, the tips in this chapter seem to work for most. They're standards for a reason—they've helped generations of parents and, in turn, will most likely work for you. As I mentioned, some of these ideas may be new to you, while others will seem like common knowledge— but it's always good to be reminded and to try the techniques again. They're especially handy if you're just beginning to play the sleep game with your first child.

Pajama Time

Change your baby into the same pajamas as a cue that it's time
for sleep. Then, each time you put on Baby's pajamas, he will
know what to expect. (Don't forget to wash them often!)

Bath Therapy

Give your baby a warm, soothing bath to relax her and
she'll be more apt to nod off afterward.

Moisturizing Massage

Put lotion on your hands to warm it up, then give your baby
a gentle massage to help relax his muscles.

Sing Baby to Sleep

Sing a lullaby or hum a simple tune to lull and comfort your baby
to sleep. *(For my favorite lullabies, see "Sweet Sounds," page 129.)*

Sound of Music

Turn on classical music or a quiet song for Baby to
listen to while she goes to sleep.

Story Time

Tell a story, read the newspaper, or just chat about
your day with your baby in a low, rhythmic voice to help
mesmerize him into dreamland.

Say Your Prayers

Repeat your favorite prayers to hypnotize your baby to snoozeville.

Say Goodnight

Use the book *Goodnight Moon* as a model for getting your
baby to sleep. Say good night to everything in baby's room—
a "lovey" (stuffed animal), a picture, a mobile, and so on.
(See "Bedtime Books," page 126.)

Rock and Roll

Swing your baby in your arms vigorously—the rocking
motion causes drowsiness.

Get Moving

Wear your baby in a front pack or sling as you move around the
house or take a walk. The motion will lead your baby to drift off.

Special Blankie

Give your baby the same blanket each time you put her down,
so she associates it with night-night time.

Close to the Heart

Buy a teddy bear that comes with the sound of a heartbeat,
and leave it in the crib with your baby. It simulates the sounds
your baby heard in the womb, which is comforting to her.
You can also buy CDs with music that sounds like Mother.

(See "Resources," page 138.)

Down the Hatch

Many babies fall asleep while nursing. If this happens, carry
your baby carefully to the crib and set him down gently so you
don't wake him. But don't leave a bottle in the crib, or the liquid
that remains in your baby's mouth may lead to cavities.

—————— ⇒ ▸ ● ◂ ⇐ ——————

Rock-a-Bye

Invest in a comfortable rocking chair and rock
your baby to sleep in it.

—————— ⇒ ▸ ● ◂ ⇐ ——————

Going Mobile

Hang a mobile over your baby's crib, wind it up,
and let him watch and listen as he dozes off.

—————— ⇒ ▸ ● ◂ ⇐ ——————

Fan Appreciation

If you have a room fan, switch it on. The sound of the fan and
the movement of the air cause many babies to go to sleep.

—————— ⇒ ▸ ● ◂ ⇐ ——————

Blow a Breeze

Blow gently on your baby's face. It helps her close her eyes and drift off. (Avoid eating onions and garlic, though!)

Soothing Sounds of Sleep

Play CDs or DVDs that have the gentle sounds of rain, the ocean, the forest, birds, and so on. They help relax baby and drown out other noises.

Pat the Baby

Put your baby in his crib, then gently pat or stroke his arms, legs, forehead, and belly.

Dark Matters

Keep the lights dim in baby's room at nighttime, and use blackout curtains during baby's daytime naps.

Teething Tricks

If your baby is teething, apply a little teething ointment
to his gums and rub them gently.

Crib Countdown

Give your baby a gentle verbal reminder that it's almost bed or
nap time, such as "Night-night time!" or "Time for beddy-bye!"
so she can adjust to the idea before you put her down.

Nap Alternates

If your baby or toddler is beginning to skip his second nap, try
alternating one nap one day, two naps the next. That way your
baby will still be tired enough to go to sleep at night. Or, just let
him skip the second nap all the time if he doesn't seem to need it.

Take a Ride

Put your baby in the car seat and drive around until she falls
asleep. This works with most babies almost every time.

Chapter 3

Tricks from Moms
Who Have Been There

○ ◗ ● ◖ ○

"No day is so bad it can't be fixed with a nap."
—*Carrie Snow*

There's no better expert in getting baby to sleep than an experienced parent. That's why I gathered the following tips from mothers who searched until they found a technique that worked. If you've tried the standards and your baby still isn't sleeping well, do something a little unusual to lull your baby to dreamland. Often parents stumble upon a method by accident and, to everyone's surprise, the trick works when tried again! Remember, one size doesn't fit all. You never know what will work with your baby until you try it!

Tune In

I played a CD of classical music softly, especially violin pieces, to get my son to sleep. (By the way, he ended up playing the violin when he got older.) —*Julaina K.*

Car Songs

I remember riding in the car while singing "The Wheels on the Bus" over and over to get my babies to calm down and fall asleep when they were fussy. —*JoAnne D.*

Accent Your Songs

I sang to my baby using different accents. The Scottish one was his favorite. —*Isobel C.*

Take Notes

I wrote down his schedule for feeding and napping and realized he was following a pattern. Then I would anticipate by a few minutes when he would be ready for a nap and put him in his crib, and he'd happily go to sleep. —*Stefany M.*

Motorized Cradle

I recommend investing in a self-rocking cradle. It saved us.
—*Melanie E.*

Keep Supplies Close

We bought a small refrigerator and kept it in the baby's room
to make that nighttime feeding as easy as possible. —*Jamie W.*

Double-Diaper

To help my baby sleep through the night, I double-diapered her,
using two cloth diapers. She woke up a lot less after I started
doing that. —*Rocio D.* (NOTE: *Today you can buy extra-thick
"overnight" diapers that serve the same purpose.*)

Time Out

Even if your baby doesn't nap well, give him a half an hour
or so in his crib so both of you can get a break. Oftentimes
he'll surprise you and end up falling asleep after half an
hour of play. —*Courtney M.*

HOW LONG DO BABIES SLEEP?

All babies are unique, with different personalities, different temperaments, and different sleep cycles. Here's a chart that shows the typical number of hours a baby sleeps—but remember, these are just statistical averages. While this may be a helpful guide, no baby sleeps exactly as a chart implies.

AGE	AVERAGE TOTAL DAILY
1 to 2 months	15 to 16 hours
3 to 5 months	15 hours
6 to 8 months	14 to 15 hours
9 to 11 months	14 hours
1 to 2 years	13 hours

TV Talk

When Jake was little, I would turn off all the lights except the TV light and turn the volume way down while I sat on the couch with him. I think he was so bored, he just fell asleep to the droning of the TV. —*Staci M.*

WHEN?	FOR HOW LONG?
2 to 3 naps plus nighttime	5 to 6 hours each stretch
2 to 3 naps plus nighttime	5 to 6 hours each stretch
2 to 3 naps plus nighttime	5 to 6 hours each stretch
2 to 3 naps plus nighttime	5 to 6 hours each stretch
1 to 2 naps plus nighttime	2 hours of naps; 11 to 12 hours at night

Temp Job

The best advice I ever got was "Keep trying." Finding the best way to get your baby to sleep just requires trial and error. For me, each baby responded differently. My son would fall asleep when I sang rap songs to him, but my daughter only responded to lullabies. —*Simonie W.*

Make a Tape

I tape-recorded the sound of my hair dryer. Then, after putting
my baby in his crib, I would play it. (NOTE: *Try tape-recording a
number of soothing sounds or white noises and playing them for
your baby at sleep time.*) —*Jana L.*

Call Your Mother

When I'm desperate, I call my mother, and we talk while
I hold and pat my baby. My mom calms me down, and soon
my baby is asleep. —*Janet S.*

Check the Checklist

Make sure you've changed him, fed him, and burped him.
Then wrap him securely in a light cotton blanket (arms and all)
and lay him halfway on his side against a small pillow.
Worked for me! —*Mary L.*

Need Noise

I couldn't live without the white-noise machine. —*Sansa B.*

Just Breathe

I always did my childbirth breathing and relaxation techniques while breast-feeding. This helped me relax, and I think it also helped my baby relax and get to sleep. —*Mary W.*

Cool Crib

I tried to make her bed a fun and happy place where she could play with her toys if she woke up or couldn't get to sleep. Just before bedtime, I'd take her into her room, and we'd play with her toys on the floor. Then I'd transfer her to the crib and include the toys we'd just played with. —*Ann P.*

Swing Time

I didn't use the mechanical swing—I used my arms and just swung her back and forth while walking around the house or standing in front of the TV. That way I got some exercise or was entertained by the talk shows. —*Kelly V.*

Take Turns

My husband and I took turns getting our baby to sleep. It wasn't a rigid pattern—whoever had the most energy went first. When one of us burned out, the other took over. —*Stephanie C.*

———— ⇒ ● ⇐ ————

Slow Down

I think I was trying too hard in the beginning to create a schedule. I had to learn to take it easy and work around the baby's patterns, and to let go of some of the other things I was trying to do. I mean, what's the hurry? This period doesn't last long, when you keep it in perspective. —*Chloe W.*

———— ⇒ ● ⇐ ————

Bonding Blanket

I always wrapped my baby in her special blanket for feedings. Then, when she fell asleep at the breast, I would use the blanket as a transition from me to the bed. —*Chris S.*

———— ⇒ ● ⇐ ————

Massage Baby's Back

Gentle stroking on the baby's back worked for us. —*Trudy C.*

———— ⚫ ————

Tummy Time

Walking the floor with the baby's tummy pressed against
my chest seemed to be comforting if she was too upset or had
a tummy ache and couldn't get to sleep. —*Connie B.*

———— ⚫ ————

Read a Book

Even though your baby is too young to understand the story,
your soothing voice can help put him to sleep. —*Vicki H.*

———— ⚫ ————

Diaper Duty

My son would fuss in the middle of the night, so I would change
his diaper and try to get him back to sleep. One night I was so
tired, I just patted him without changing his diaper, and he went
right back to sleep! Try not to change the diaper in the middle
of his sleep period if you can get away with it. —*Kathy J.*

———— ⚫ ————

COPING WITH COLIC

A colicky baby can add extra stress for a new parent, especially if he's interfering with everyone's sleep. If your baby cries regularly for long periods (over three hours), it's usually because of an immature nervous system that is affecting his tummy and digestive system. The good news is that most babies outgrow colic by three months. The bad news is that it's difficult to cope with. Here are some tips for handling colic until your baby matures:

- Swing or rock him. Movement seems to help calm the fussiness.

- Play music or sing. Soft sounds and white noise seem to distract colicky babies.

- Massage him. Give him a back or tummy rub, to help the digestive system and process the food, in case it has become stuck.

- Switch formula. Sometimes the milk doesn't agree with your baby, so try another type of formula.

- Cut out gassy foods. Eliminate anything from your diet that seems to affect your baby after nursing, such as caffeine, cabbage, beans, etc.

- Check with your doctor. If you've tried several remedies and your baby continues to cry, check with your doctor to see if something else is causing the problem.

Day vs. Night

My Lamaze teacher said babies have a hard time distinguishing day from night in the beginning, because they're rocked during the day as we move around, and when we lie down to sleep, they wake up and party. So I made an effort to reverse that by rocking him at night to get him to sleep, and keeping him busy during the day. After three or four days of that, he seemed to understand that night was sleeptime and day was fun time. —*Carole P.*

Note about Naps

I was always told never to wake a sleeping baby, but my son took long naps and didn't sleep well at night. I started gently waking him after three hours of nap time, and that made a big difference in his nighttime sleep. —*Rena L.*

Bore Her to Sleep

I used to just talk in a quiet voice and tell her everything that was happening, all my problems, just nonstop chatter with lots of repetition. I got to vent, while she got to sleep. —*Ann C.*

Bed Play

If your baby has been put down for bedtime, but you can hear him talking or playing in the crib, leave him alone. He'll soon grow tired and fall asleep on his own. —*Tracy P.*

———— ⋗ ● ⋖ ————

Off-Key

Sing to your baby. It helps if you sing off-key, because the baby will go to sleep in self-defense. At least, it worked for me. —*Deanna M.*

———— ⋗ ● ⋖ ————

Early Intervention

Contrary to most advice, which says not to go into baby's room unless he's really crying, I found that if I went in when he just began making those little waking noises and patted him, he'd eventually go back to sleep on his own. —*Julie L.*

———— ⋗ ● ⋖ ————

CONVERSATIONS WITH YOUR CUTIE-PIE

If you don't know what to say to your baby, here are some conversation topics that will surely lull him to sleep.

- Recount your busy day

- Tell your baby how special he is

- Talk about the weather

- Share the latest gossip

- Discuss current events

- Complain about gas prices

- Mention some child-rearing techniques you might try

- Open up about your hopes and dreams for your child—and yourself!

- Fantasize about the perfect vacation

- Analyze your relatives

- Brainstorm plans for house renovations

- Giggle about your partner's quirks

- Discuss politics, religion, and sex—things you can't discuss with other people

Change the Clock

In the beginning, I thought my baby would sleep better if I kept him awake a little longer when he showed signs of sleep. But when I realized that my baby was really overtired at that point, I put him down half an hour earlier than his regular schedule. Solved the problem immediately! —*Natalie L.*

Bed Bounce

I learned this from my nanny. She placed both hands on the crib mattress, on either side of my baby, and gently bounced the bed until he fell asleep.—*Bonnie J.*

Sling Baby

I put my baby in a sling and went on with my daily routines. She loved the rhythm and movement, the warmth of my body, and the sense of security of being close to me. —*Ashley M.*

Attitude Adjustment

Focus on the positive. Appreciate how much your baby *is* sleeping, instead of how little. Think about how much she's changing and growing and developing, and be confident that she will sleep longer over time. In the meantime, if your baby is awake a lot and you need catch-up sleep, hire a babysitter to watch him while you take a nap. —*Susan G.*

Don't Force It

Sometimes your baby just isn't sleepy. This often seems to happen when she's learning new skills. After you've given it a try, give up, do some kind of activity, and then try again. Instead of becoming frustrated and upset and forcing her to nap or sleep, stop.—*Elizabeth M.*

Car Seat Security

My son needed motion to fall asleep, so we would drive him around in his car seat. When he dozed off, we just unsnapped the seat from the base, brought it in into the house, and let him sleep in it. I think the harness gave him the same feeling of security that swaddling does for young infants. —*Staci M.*

Repeat Rituals

I had a ritual that when I put my baby down, I would
repeat in a sing-song voice exactly the same thing each time.
Mine went like this: "Bedtime, Bradley. Here's your dee-dee
(his blanket). Here's your Elmo (his lovey). Kiss-kiss, night-night.
Love you, Bradley." After a few nights, it seemed to work like
a hypnotic suggestion. —*Sue W.*

Counting Sheep

My son Cole has this sheep toy that plays soothing sounds,
like waves. I read a book, then turn on the sheep and a turtle
that lights stars on the ceiling. That seems to quiet him down.
—*Amy S.* (NOTE: *There are several baby accessories that help get
baby to sleep. See "Resources," page 138, for recommendations.*)

Music for Babies

I have this CD of soothing music for babies that I play
consistently. I put him up on my shoulder, dim the lights,
and rock him. He knows it's his "sleepy music." —*Sally P.*
(NOTE: *See "Resources," page 138, for suggestions.*)

Formula Food

My grandmother told me to bathe my babies in warm water,
then give them their last bottles with a little bit of baby cereal
in them. I had to make the holes a little larger so they could
suck, but it made them feel full and content. And they slept
through the night. —*Rachel M.*

Clean and Carry

When I brought my baby home from the hospital and couldn't
get him to sleep, my mom suggested that I vacuum with one arm
and hold the baby with the other. The motion and the sound of
the vacuum were soothing. —*Candi W.*

Laundry Load

The only way I could get my extremely colicky baby
to sleep was while doing laundry. I would put him in his
infant car seat on top of the dryer as I folded clothes. The
motion and noise seemed to get him to sleep—and I sure
did get a lot of laundry done! —*Rachel G.*

Up and Down

The *only* way we were able to get Julia to sleep for the first
nine months of her life was to walk up and down the stairs—
over and over, up and down—until she finally fell asleep.
My mom, hubby, and I took turns. —*Cyrena W.*

Sleep School

I had twins, so getting them to sleep was especially
important to me. We did what we called "sleep school."
We put our babies down with something they could pick up and
use themselves, such as a pacifier, rattle, or silky (a piece of silk
fabric). When they cried, we'd go back in at three minutes, then
wait six minutes, then nine, then twelve, until they were asleep.
The next night, we did it in increments of five, then ten, fifteen,
etc. When this was done consistently, they learned that they
were safe and that we were there for them, so they could
relax and go to sleep. —*Bonnie D.*

Dad vs. Mom

Sometimes when one parent has trouble getting baby to sleep,
the other parent does the trick. I realized that my husband, Dave,
and I have different techniques, and what works for him (patting
her back increasingly slowly and lightly) doesn't work for me.
I sit and rock her, and she goes to sleep. So try to understand that
every relationship with the baby is different, and what works for
some doesn't necessarily work for others. —*Shauna M.*

───── ⤖ ● ⤆ ─────

Cricket Sounds

I found that the sound of crickets outside the window
helped my baby get to sleep. When we traveled with her,
at night I had to make cricket sounds to get her to sleep.
I don't know if you can buy a CD with cricket noises,
but if it's available, it's worth a try! —*Patty G.*

───── ⤖ ● ⤆ ─────

Park at the Park

I'll either walk my baby to the park in his stroller or drive him
there, both of which get him to sleep. While he sleeps in the shade,
I catch up on writing or paperwork. —*Amy M.*

───── ⤖ ● ⤆ ─────

ON THE ROAD: TRAVELING AND SLEEP

Here are some tips for helping your baby sleep better while you're taking a trip.

- Let your baby sleep in bed with you to make him feel secure in a strange place.

- Ask the hotel to provide a crib for your baby—many have cribs available.

- Bring along a bedtime transitional object, such as a stuffed animal, lovey, familiar blanket, or pacifier.

- Try to maintain your usual rituals while traveling, such as regular mealtimes, playtime, and bedtime.

- If you have to break your normal routine, return to it as soon as you return home.

Baby Ball

I hold my baby in my arms all snuggled up, then sit on a big ball and bounce. My baby goes to sleep, while I get a good workout. —*Brie F.*

Before Birth

I played certain classical music to my pregnant belly every day, so after my son was born, I would just put on that same CD and he would fall asleep! —*Tessa L.*

* * *

Peek-a-Baby

My grandson pulls a small scrap of blanket over his eyes or next to his face, and it calms him down and puts him out. You might try draping a piece of fabric over your baby's forehead and eyes to help him shut down. —*Shirley D.* (NOTE: *Make sure the piece of fabric is less than 5 inches square to prevent suffocation.*)

* * *

Bed Check

The only thing that's worked for me so far is listening for those little noises that come just before my son wakes up, then going into the room and cuddling with him or patting him through the transition phase so he never really awakens. The idea is for him to learn to put himself back to sleep. —*Jennifer A.*

* * *

Elmo's Asleep

My son covers up Elmo with a little blanket and says
good night, and if Elmo is asleep, he thinks everyone is going
to sleep—so he goes to sleep! You might try this with your
baby's favorite stuffed animal. —*Amy S.*

Tummy to Tummy

I used to put my baby on my tummy, lie down, and let her
go to sleep that way. —*Zoe G.*

Book 'Em

Here's a strange one, but it worked on my nephew.
He would only go to sleep if you patted him on the back for
what seemed like a long time. We discovered that you could pat
him slower for a few minutes, put a book on his back to imitate
the feel of the hand, and then leave. We'd remove the book
after he fell asleep. It worked great. —*Anne G.*

Dry Shower

Take a "dry shower." Stand in the bathroom (but not *in* the shower) with the shower running while holding your baby. The running water imitates the sounds of the womb. —*Kelly G.*

Cold Feet

I found that if I covered my baby's feet with soft little socks, he fell asleep faster. —*Sue W.*

Ticking Heart

Wrap a clock in something soft and lay it near the baby so she can hear the muffled ticking. She will be comforted, because it sounds like mother's heartbeat. —*Kay A.*

Chill Out

If I'm tense when trying to put my fifteen-month-old son to sleep, the whole endeavor is pointless. So I take a few deep breaths and consciously relax my body. His little body almost immediately reacts the same way. —*Arianna O.*

Warm the Wipes

My baby wouldn't go back to sleep after I changed him. I finally figured out that the wipes were too cold! I bought a wipe warmer, and that made a huge difference. —*Melissa A.*

Water Works

I found that running water put my baby to sleep, so I put my baby's port-a-crib in the kitchen and turned on the faucet for a little while. —*Gail P.*

Bike Stand

I used to hop onto the stationary bike wearing my baby in a front pack, then exercise my pregnancy weight off while my baby nodded off. —*Mia. T.*

Dishwasher Wonder

One day I had my baby in his infant seat on the floor a few
feet from the dishwasher. After loading the dishwasher, I turned
it on, and moments later my baby was asleep. I started using this
technique whenever my daughter couldn't get to sleep in her crib.
(Just make sure your baby isn't too close to the dishwasher,
which can give off steam.) —*Barbara S.*

Fake Sleep

This may sound strange, but when I was exhausted, I would just
lay in my bed with my baby next to me and pretend to sleep.
Pretty soon he'd be asleep too! —*Holly K.*

Sandman Stroke

I would take my finger and stroke my baby's forehead down
toward his nose several times until he fell asleep. —*Barbara G.*

Baby Whispering

Whispering—not singing—songs in her ear worked.
"Hush, Little Baby" was her favorite. —*Gay C.*

Pat the Bottom

Pat your baby firmly—not too firmly, just pressure—
on her bottom instead of her back. —*Deanna M.*

Swing Seat

Put your baby in a car seat with handles and swing or
rock her back and forth. —*Donna B.*

Knit One

I'd knit as my daughter watched from her swing. The clicking
needles seemed to hypnotize her to sleep. —*Carole P.*

Grandma's Fussbuster

I know this sounds crazy, but we got a CD called
Grandma's Fussbuster, which plays sounds like "The Hoover
Hustle" (vacuum-cleaner noises), "Hair Today, Gone Tomorrow"
(the hair dryer), and "Someone to Wash over Me"
(the dishwasher). I swear by it. —*Elizabeth G.*
(NOTE: *See "Resources," page 138.*)

Take a Stroll

Riding in the stroller always put my baby to sleep after she was fed, but when the weather turned cold and rainy, I couldn't use the stroller outside anymore, so I started pushing it around in the house. I must have looked ridiculous, but whatever it takes!
—*Jacqueline H.*

Blanket Warmer

We would warm the blanket in the dryer, then wrap her up and give her last bottle for the night. It really relaxed her. As she got drowsy, we would remove the blanket and put her in her crib. —*Lima C.*

Smooth as Silk

Use a blanket with a satin trim. The soft, silky feeling seems to help babies sleep. —*Patty G.*

Light the Night

Hang up colored lights around the room for a soothing atmosphere, instead of using a night-light. —*Stefany M.*

―――― ⇒ ⊃● ● ●⊂ ⇐ ――――

Mommy's Scent

Lightly spray a favorite blanket or shirt with the perfume you wear to make your baby think you're nearby. —*Carole P.*

―――― ⇒ ⊃● ● ●⊂ ⇐ ――――

Movie Time

I used a Winnie the Pooh ceiling projector to mesmerize our baby while he's lying on his back in the crib. —*Anne G.*

―――― ⇒ ⊃● ● ●⊂ ⇐ ――――

Crib Corner

My baby would always scoot to the corner of the crib before falling asleep. I think having something to rest his head against made him feel like he was back in the womb. —*Ann P.*

―――― ⇒ ⊃● ● ●⊂ ⇐ ――――

Warm Hands

I have cold hands, and that used to keep my baby from falling asleep. My mother-in-law told me to warm my hands first before I held him, and it worked. He "warmed" to my touch and fell asleep. —*Carole P.*

Sleeping at the Breast

My baby would doze off during the first half of her feeding, so I would put her down, but then she'd wake up a short time later because she was still hungry. So I tried to keep her awake by playing with her hands, talking to her, etc., so she'd get a full feeding before becoming too drowsy. —*Staci M.*

Allergic Reaction

I didn't realize that my baby became gassy when I ate certain foods (beans, to be exact). Since I was breast-feeding, these kept him from getting to sleep. When I finally figured out what was causing the problem and stopped eating those foods, he fell asleep much more easily. —*Sue W.*

Warm to Cool

I thought I was supposed to warm the bottle for my baby,
but one time when I couldn't and just gave it to him cold, he
had much less tummy upset and therefore got to sleep better.
Try changing the temperature of the milk (if you can)
and see what happens. —*Barbara S.*

Peppermint Tea

My doctor said that peppermint has an ingredient that helps
relieve gas, and recommended that I give my baby warm, weak
peppermint tea. It seemed to help a lot. —*JoAnne D.*

Ear Tracing

Try running your finger along the inside of the outer ear
(not inside!) to put babies to sleep. —*Bernadette G.*

MIDNIGHT DISTRACTIONS

Here are some things to do when you're up with your wide-awake baby in the middle of the night.

- Watch an old movie.

- Read a book.

- Catch up on your magazine pile.

- Work off some of that baby weight by walking your baby or using the StairMaster.

- Chat on the phone with another middle-of-the-night mother or single friend who is likely to be up at that hour.

- Brainstorm new project ideas for your work or favorite hobby.

- Invest in TiVo so you can watch shows you don't get to see during regular broadcasts.

- Organize your iTunes playlists.

- Do a crossword puzzle.

- Make a list of tomorrow's plans.

- Work on a problem you're having.

- Read your e-mail.

- Text message friends.

- Write thank-you notes or letters.

- Plan your baby's future.

Chapter 4

Dads on Duty
Game Plan

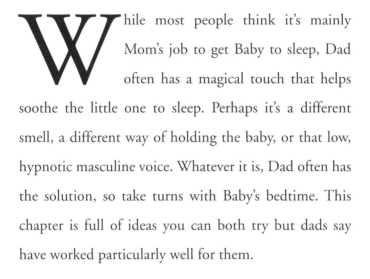

"Anyone who thinks the art of conversation is dead ought to tell
a child to go to bed." —*Robert Gallagher*

While most people think it's mainly Mom's job to get Baby to sleep, Dad often has a magical touch that helps soothe the little one to sleep. Perhaps it's a different smell, a different way of holding the baby, or that low, hypnotic masculine voice. Whatever it is, Dad often has the solution, so take turns with Baby's bedtime. This chapter is full of ideas you can both try but dads say have worked particularly well for them.

Wear Them Out

What worked for us was just plain wearing them down with play time, but that usually wore me down, too! —*Doug D.*

―――― ⋙ ● ⋘ ――――

"Buddy Boy"

Make up your own song and sing it to your baby.
I used to sing the words "Buddy Boy" over and over until my grandson fell asleep —*Ed P.*

―――― ⋙ ● ⋘ ――――

Oil the Door

The door would squeak every time we opened it,
which would wake the baby, so I oiled the door. No more noise,
no more wake-ups. —*Mike M.*

―――― ⋙ ● ⋘ ――――

Toys in Babeland

Put some of your baby's favorite toys in the crib so when he
wakes up, he can play with his toys until he feels sleepy again.
(Just make sure the toys are safe ones.) —*Chad A.*

―――― ⋙ ● ⋘ ――――

SONGS FOR DADS TO SING

(Even If They Don't Know All the Words)

"99 Bottles of Beer on the Wall"

"Who Let the Dogs Out?"

"Take Me Out to the Ball Game"

"Don't Worry, Be Happy"

"A Pirate's Life for Me"
 (from the *Pirates of the Caribbean* ride)

"We Are the Champions"

"Eye of the Tiger"

"Where Everybody Knows Your Name"
 (theme from *Cheers*)

Notre Dame fight song

"Stairway to Heaven"

The Alphabet Song

Bottles of Beer?

Singing "99 Bottles of Beer on the Wall" often did the trick.
It sometimes took 199 or 299, though. —*Geoff P.*

Tickle Teddy

A vibrating toy, such as a teddy bear, will help a baby get to sleep.
—*Mike M.*

Chill the Pacifier

When my son was teething, he didn't sleep well,
so I would put his pacifier in the freezer to get it nice and cold,
then give it to him. —*Geoff P.*

Snack Time

To keep him from waking in the night, we fed our son
more during the day. —*Ray C.*

Dad Style

My wife and I hold our son differently. She holds him close,
while I tend to hold him like a football, across my arm,
to get him to sleep. —*Len S.*

Bundle Blanket

We got a blanket-sleeper. You put the kid inside and zip it up, and when he kicks, he can't kick the blanket off and wake up. Seems to make him feel all cozy and warm and safe. —*Dennis B.*

Minimize the Monitor

Turn down the baby monitor when you go to bed, so you don't hear every little wake-up sound. You'll still hear the big ones that mean "Come and get me!" but you'll sleep through the little ones, when your baby may be awake but he's content and will probably go back to sleep on his own. —*Dave M.*

Vibrating Crib

I broke down and got a vibrating baby bed. My wife was against it, but we both tried rocking him, and that really didn't work. A friend of mine said it was great, and sure enough, it worked like a charm. —*Patrick G.*

Light and Dark

While holding the baby, move back and forth between
light and dark rooms. It causes the baby to close her eyes
and eventually fall asleep. —*Wayne Y.*

———— ⋙ ◦ ⋘ ————

Countdown to Crib

I started this early on and kept it up with all my kids. It's called
the Crib Countdown. When it's time for bed, I count from one to
ten and match an action to each number. Here's my countdown:
"One hug" (I hug him and carry him off to bed). "Two kisses"
(one on each cheek). "Three night-nights" (I wave three times).
"Four corners" (I tuck in each of the four corners of the blanket).
"Five fingers" (I count his fingers). "Six toys" (I count his toys
nearby). "Seven belly rubs" (I rub his belly). "Eight hair strokes"
(I stroke his hair). "Nine pats" (I pat him lightly). And "ten steps"
(I step backward out of the room, counting to ten). —*Mike M.*

———— ⋙ ◦ ⋘ ————

Lay on Hands

All I had to do was place my big, warm hand on my son's back,
and he would immediately relax and fall back asleep. My wife
thought I had the magic touch. —*Geoff P.*

Lower Your Voice

I think it was my deep voice that got our baby to sleep.
All I had to do was talk to him or sing a little, and he'd fall asleep.
—*Charles M.*

Mickey Mouse

Take him to Disneyland for the day. He'll sleep like a log all night.
—*Brad E.*

Let It Rain

Use a "rain stick" with your baby. It's a tube made from dried cactus, with little seeds inside that make the sound of rain when you turn it over and over. You can find them at toy and science stores, or make your own. —*David R.*

A Little Shot

My dad used to dip his finger in his whiskey and let us suck on it. I think a better idea is to take a shot of whiskey yourself. —*Greg P.*

DAD'S DISCS
Sleep Songs Recorded by Men, for Men

Papa's Lullaby by Ellipsis Arts

Daddies Sing Goodnight: A Father's Collection of Sleepytime Songs by Sugar Hill

Somebody's Daddy: Lullabies for Dad by Joe Milton

Daddy's Lullabies by Re Bops

Sing Me to Sleep Daddy by Brentwood

Good Night by Jim Weiss

Golden Slumbers: A Father's Lullaby by Norman Brown, et al.

Songs from a Parent to a Child by Art Garfunkel

Bedtime with the Beatles by Jason Falkner

Disney's Lullaby Album by Fred Mollin, Greg Diakun, and Disney

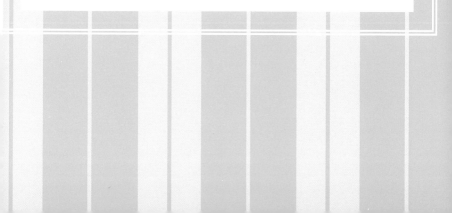

Chapter 5
Old Wives' Tales

○) ● (○

"The only thing worth stealing is a kiss from a sleeping child."
—*Joe Houldsworth*

D id you ever hear the one about getting your baby to sleep by placing an onion near his crib? I can only imagine that the noxious smell of the onion causes him to close his eyes in self-defense! Many old wives' tales are based on superstition, but some have roots in long-standing knowledge and experience that's been passed on from generation to generation, and offer well-established advice, such as breast-feeding. While I can't medically guarantee the success of all of them, some parents and grandparents I know swear by these traditional methods. This chapter includes some of my favorites I've heard over the years.

Creeping Cats

Rumor once had it cats can suck the air from your baby's mouth. That's just not possible, but the story persists, probably because cats are curious about the new addition, and they may smell the milk. You don't have to put Fluffy up for adoption just because you have a new baby, but do make sure not to leave your baby unattended with cats, dogs, or other pets, because they can be unpredictable and even jealous of the new baby.

Thumb-Sucking Update

In the old days, parents used to bind their babies' arms so they couldn't bend them at the elbow and therefore couldn't suck their thumbs. Parents were concerned that thumb-sucking led to buck teeth and a dependency on the habit. But sucking is a basic need in babies, and most begin sucking their thumbs even in the uterus. Babies have distinct preferences and either choose their thumbs or a pacifier for extra sucking. Studies today indicate that sucking may help prevent SIDS and does not cause dental problems, so let him suck if he wants to.

Turn Up the Volume

If you've ever been hushed around a sleeping baby, that's due to the conventional thinking that baby needs absolute quiet to get to sleep. But this simply isn't true for all babies. Some parents swear that their babies fall asleep when it's noisy—at loud parties, restaurants, or with the TV on. One theory is that if baby is overstimulated, she "shuts down" and goes to sleep, so absolute quiet may not work for her.

Swing Fast and Low

While many people recommend that you swing your baby back and forth to get him to sleep, some parents used to be a little too vigorous in the past, and shook their babies to quiet them. Now we know that this may cause Shaken Baby Syndrome, a disorder that can cause brain damage, so you need to be careful when swinging or moving your baby.

Upright Is Right

Most parents are more comfortable feeding Baby while holding her sideways across the abdomen. But Grandma used to recommend holding baby upright while feeding her, saying it helped her process the food better, and therefore sleep better. While this position may be more awkward, it's not harmful, and it just might work.

Breast Milk Is Better

For a while, women were encouraged to bottle-feed their babies because their milk might not be rich enough or plentiful enough, so many mothers stopped breast-feeding and switched to bottles. Today we know that breast milk is best for Baby. It's easier to digest and therefore causes fewer spit-ups and tummy aches and less gas. The act of sucking on a breast as opposed to a bottle nipple aids in Baby's digestion, by creating waves than push the milk down and reduce the intake of air. Avoid bottle-feeding if you want your baby to sleep well at night.

Diaper-Rash Cure

A diaper rash will keep your baby from sleeping well.
Luckily, there are several products on the market that will help
prevent diaper rash or clear it up, such as Desitin, Burt's Baby Bee
Diaper Ointment, and Boudreaux's Butt Paste. But to clear up the
irritation fast, Grandma often used to crush Tums tablets and mix
them with diaper-rash cream, then rub the mixture on
baby's bottom after each diaper change.

Spritz to Sleep

In the past, parents thought certain smells helped Baby sleep, such
as the scent of roses or lavender. Today you can buy products with
scents, such as Fussy Mussy Spritzer, (which smells like roses), then
spray it on Baby's face, avoiding the eyes. Or try an aromatherapy
candle (just make sure it's placed in a safe area).

Gripe Water

Gripe water is a homeopathic remedy that contains chamomile, fennel, caraway, ginger, peppermint, lemon balm, aloe, and vegetable carbon. Give it to your baby, following the directions on the bottle, to calm him and help him sleep.

Turn Around

Some say that if you turn your baby upside-down, with her feet at the head and her head at the foot of the bed, she'll fall asleep thanks to the new environment.

Pumpkin for Pun'kin

Parents would once offer their babies strained pumpkin, slightly sweetened, to get baby to sleep. It probably worked because pumpkin is high in carbohydrates, which release serotonins, a natural sleep enhancer.

Add a Plant

In the old days, parents thought babies breathed better if there was a plant in the room to help provide extra oxygen. Although it isn't likely that there will be a lack of oxygen in your baby's room, putting a nontoxic plant in her room can't hurt.

A Whiff of Onion

In the past, some mothers would take a yellow onion, chop it up, and place it in container with a lid near Baby's bed, then let out a whiff of the onion to get baby to sleep. I would think the strong smell would wake the baby, but other cultures sometimes use this method, so it may be worth a try.

Bedtime Banana

I found an old baby book that suggested you serve your baby mashed banana at bedtime to cause drowsiness. We now know that bananas contain L-triptophan, which aids in sleep, so they may have been onto something.

Avoid Moonlight

A common old wives' tale claims that bright moonlight shining into your baby's face can keep him from sleeping, much like a night-light that's too bright. While it may not be the moonlight that's keeping Baby awake, it makes sense that anything shining in Baby's face or too bright in the room can prevent sleep. Draw the curtains and check the strength of the night-light to make sure this isn't what's keeping your baby from sleep.

Toe Wiggling

Some old wives' tales recommend wiggling your baby's toes to help her relax and get her to sleep, but the reason has been lost over time. Still, there may be something to this. Today, many use reflexology for the same thing, with the belief that toe wiggling helps channel energy that causes relaxation.

Tummy Rub

Many believe that gently massaging baby's stomach in
clockwise circles will help with digestion, which leads to sleep.
The clockwise direction is thought to relieve blockage in the colon,
but back then it was probably discovered through trial and error,
and then passed down through generations.

Stop Worrying!

Grandmother often advised the new mother not to worry,
knowing that eventually baby will go to sleep. That was probably
easy for her to say in retrospect, but the advice is still solid:
Relax and keep your focus on the big picture. Soon your baby
will outgrow this problem and be into something else. Before you
know it, your baby will be all grown up! In the meantime—
here's the most important tip of all: Enjoy your baby!

Chapter 6

Treasured Tips
from Other Cultures

"Oh sleep! It is a gentle thing, Beloved from pole to pole."
—*Samuel Taylor Coleridge*

When babies around the world begin to talk, they speak different languages, but when they won't go to sleep, it's the exact same problem worldwide. While many techniques are the same everywhere, such as rocking and singing to baby, many cultures also have their own special tricks and different approaches to sleep. Learn what parents around the globe do to get their babies to sleep—and try a couple of these techniques in your own home.

India

Parents play Indian CDs—everything from Bollywood hits to sitar songs—on low volume and sing along to help their babies go to sleep. Invest in some international music to play for your baby. Some parents turn traditional folktales into songs and sing them to their babies. Follow their lead and sing *Goodnight Moon* or *The Night Before Christmas.*

Another technique used in India is a swing on a string. Parents attach a string to a small rocking bed and pull it from a distance while humming a special tune called a *lorrie.*

In India, the Ayurvedic culture believes that the combination of the body, mind, and soul work together to prevent health problems. One method mothers use is massage on their baby's tummies with a ball of dough coated with a little almond oil and turmeric, to help baby's digestion and calm him to sleep.

GLOBAL BEATS

*Check out these CDs, which are specially designed to get baby to
sleep in any language.*

> *World Music for Little Ears* by Ellipsis Arts
> *World of Love: Authentic Lullabies from*
> *Around the World* by Ellipsis Arts
> *The Planet Sleeps* by Sony
> *Latin Lullaby* by Ellipsis Arts
> *Mother Earth Lullaby* by Ellipsis Arts
> *African Lullaby* by Ellipsis Arts
> *Celtic Lullaby* by Ellipsis Arts

SAY "GOOD NIGHT" SEVENTEEN MORE TIMES

Chinese: *Jóutáu*

Czech: *Dobrou noc*

Danish: *God nat*

French: *Bonne nuit*

Gaelic: *Oíche mhaith*

German: *Gute nacht*

Greek: *Kaliníhta*

Hebrew: *Aila tov*

Indonesian: *Selamat malam*

Italian: *Buonanotte*

Japanese: *Oyasumi*

Portuguese: *Boa noite*

Russian: *Spokojnoj noči*

Spanish: *Buenas noches*

Swahili: *Lala salama*

Swedish: *God natt*

Welsh: *Nos da*

Iran

Parents often give their babies oil baths to relax them.
Just add a little baby oil to the bathwater and massage him
with the oily water.

Another popular technique is a leg cradle. The parent stretches
out on the floor or couch, sets a pillow on top of her legs, places
the baby on the pillow, and rocks her legs back and forth.

Algeria

Mothers wrap their babies in towels and tie them to their backs,
then walk around doing their chores while humming. (Just be sure
the towel is secure, so the baby won't fall out!)

Scotland

The Scots mix a little oatmeal gruel with honey to get Baby
to sleep. (NOTE: *Today it's not recommended that children under the
age of one have honey, because of the risk for botulism. So if you want
to try this one, use oatmeal without the honey, or add a
hint of sugar if you must.*)

The Balkans

Parents offer their babies buttermilk half an hour before
bedtime to soothe their tummies for sleep.

China

In Chinese culture, parents pat their babies' backs and
repeat the soothing sound "oho" softly.

Some parents put their babies in a cart called a *yaoche,*
hold one end, and gently shake it.

Other mothers place their babies on their outstretched
legs and rock the legs back and forth.

Chinese parents chop ginseng and orange peel, mix them
with honey, and feed the mixture to baby to get her to sleep.
(NOTE: *Today it's not recommended that children under the age
of one have honey, because of the risk for botulism.)*

FENG SHUI

Ancient Chinese wisdom recommends that parents use feng shui to help their babies sleep. You might find that a few small changes to the placement of your baby's furniture make all the difference.

- For proper feng shui, have your baby sleep with her head pointing south.

- Place the bed so your baby can see the door, but not so she is directly across from it, or you may obstruct the smooth flow of chi. The best position for the bed is diagonal to the door, and her feet should be aimed in that direction.

- Avoid having your baby sleep under a window, to prevent a bad impact on her chi.

- Don't place pictures of water in the room; they cause insomnia and attract bad luck.

- Don't hang mirrors in the bedroom, because reflections disturb the healing process when your baby's body is at rest.

- The bed should not be placed under a beam, which can cause headaches and tension.

- Don't keep electronic items like TVs, music systems, or computers near the baby's bed. The electromagnetic radiation may disturb sleep, so unplug or cover them at night.

- Place an aromatherapy candle on a plate with flowers in water in the northeast corner of the room to ensure a good night's rest. (**NOTE:** Never leave a burning candle unattended.)

Tibet

In the Buddhist tradition, parents lay their babies in the crib with their heads pointing south for a more refreshing sleep.

———— ✦ ● ✦ ————

American Indian

Native Americans wore their babies in baby boards—flat boards made of compressed wood, beaded and decorated, and padded for comfort. Baby boards are traditional in most Indian cultures to provide security and protection for baby while he nods off to sleep. They've been used for centuries and are still in use today. Babies are wrapped and tied in, which simulates being held and cuddled. A donut shape is added for head support and to prevent the head from flattening.

Some add wild rosewood to protect the baby from bad spirits, and shells and beads fringe the board to create a soothing, quieting effect when baby is rocked.

———— ✦ ● ✦ ————

Universally Appealing

In many countries, parents give their babies a few sips of warm tea with chamomile or mint and sugar to get baby to doze off.

In some cultures, parents lay the baby in a quiet area, open a window, or turn on a fan, and hang some wind chimes for the baby to listen to.

Many cultures rub baby's belly gently with warm olive oil to release gas buildup and calm her.

Often parents around the world, including in the United States, feed the baby cereal or fruit to help fill her up, hoping she will go to sleep when her tummy is full. While doctors believe this doesn't really work, some parents swear by it.

Some parents run water from the faucet so baby can hear it. As the water drips into a pot, the sounds change, lulling the baby to sleep.

Chapter 7

If All Else Fails

"Fatigue is the best pillow." —*Benjamin Franklin*

Once in a while, it may seem like everything you've tried just won't work and you've reached the end of your rope. This will wear you down quickly, and we all know sleep deprivation can make ordinary irritations seem even worse. Luckily, I've still got a few tricks left. When you think you've tried it all, it's time to step it up a notch and try these tips, which worked for other desperate parents. Your baby may be sleepless, but the situation is never hopeless!

Hire Help

It may sound like cheating, but if you're running low on patience and energy, hire a sitter to come in and try to get your baby to sleep while you take a break.

Sleep Smells

Lay your baby in the crib with the robe you wear when breast-feeding, so your baby is reminded of you and will relax to sleep. Or buy some similar fabric, express a little milk on it, and put it in the crib with your baby.

Bedtime Snack

There's an amino acid called tryptophan in foods like milk and turkey that produces serotonin, a chemical that helps the body relax, in the brain. So try a few teaspoons of turkey baby food with milk.

It's the Air

Following the instructions that come with the appliance,
turn on a humidifier without the water, so it makes a soft noise.
(Just be sure it's safe to use without water.)

Short-Term Cry It Out

Some babies need a few minutes to tire themselves through crying.
Let your baby cry no more than ten to fifteen minutes, then go in
to soothe her. Keep repeating until she falls asleep.

Settle the Stomach

After checking with your doctor for approval and dosage,
try giving your baby a little antacid, if he seems to have an upset
stomach that's keeping him from sleeping.

IN GOOD COMPANY

You're never the only mom or dad up at night with a sleepless child. Check out these entertaining baby-themed movies while you're wishing you both were fast asleep.

Baby Boom, with Diane Keaton

Three Men and a Baby, with Tom Selleck

She's Having a Baby, with Kevin Bacon

Look Who's Talking, with John Travolta

Father of the Bride 2, with Steve Martin

Nine Months, with Hugh Grant

My Baby's Daddy, with Anthony Anderson

Daddy Day Care, with Eddie Murphy

One for the Bed

Some babies need to be "topped off" to keep them from
waking in the night. Gently rouse your baby before you go to bed,
give her one last feeding, and return her to bed, full and drowsy.

Warm the Bed

Lay a heating pad on the bed before putting baby down,
then remove it and lay your baby on the warm bed. You can
also use an iron or a hot-water bottle.

Call for Help

If you've really given it your best shot and your baby
is still not sleeping through the night, then it may be time
to consult your child's physician again, or to consider
a sleep specialist.

Chapter 8

Special Care:
Soothing Products for Baby

"Always kiss your children good night—even if they're already asleep."
—*H. Jackson Brown, Jr.*

Luckily for the sleepless parent and baby, there are a number of products designed to break that wakeful cycle and get baby to sleep. Here are some that experienced parents have tried and found effective.

Baby Sleeping Bag

Slip your baby into a baby sleeping bag—half sleeper, half bag—to keep her from kicking off the covers and getting cold in the night.

(My favorites: www.babyinabag.com, www.sleephuggers.com)

Baby Lovey Blanket

Buy a small, super-soft blanket with stuffed-animal head attached for baby to use as a self-comforter in the night.

(My favorite: www.baby-blankets.us)

Slumber Bear

Provide a stuffed bear that plays lullabies, heartbeat sounds, even digestion noises, reminding baby of the womb.

(My favorites: Slumber Bear at www.dreamtimebaby.com and the Original Slumber Bear at www.drugstore.com)

Swaddle Blanket

Try a preformed swaddling blanket to wrap up your baby and calm him down.

(My favorites: Baby Swaddler at www.thebabyswaddler.com and Easy Wrap Swaddler at www.babythisbabythat.com)

White-Noise Machine

Turn on a white-noise machine that helps mask other sounds.
It will relax your baby and soothe her to sleep.
*(My favorites: Sleep Sheep at www.sleepwellbaby.com and
Baby's First White Noise CD at www.purewhitenoise.com)*

Baby Motion Beds

Some parents of especially fussy babies swear by motion
beds and bassinets that gently rock babies to sleep.
(My favorite: Amby Baby Motion Bed at www.ambybaby.com)

Sleep Wedges and Forms

These specially designed wedges and forms help keep
baby from turning over and waking up.
(My favorite: Baby Be Safe Sleep Wedge at www.gallerybcentral.com)

Fleece Crib Sheets

Sometimes extra-cozy crib sheets can comfort baby to sleep.
Warmer to begin with, they prevent baby from startling awake
at the touch of cold sheets when you put him in bed.
(My favorites: www.fleecebaby.com and www.dreamsoftbedware.com)

Baby Massage Kit

Make massaging your baby more fun by using kits
that come with oils and massage techniques. Or make
your own, by combining two tablespoons of safflower
oil and five drops of lavender-essence oil.
(My favorite: www.mamaandme.com)

⟶ ⟩⟩ ● ⟨⟨ ⟵

Sleep Nest

If you prefer to have your baby in bed with you,
buy a sleep nest that keeps your baby safe from being
smothered by your body during the night.
(My favorite: Snuggle Nest at www.mommysthinkin.com)

⟶ ⟩⟩ ● ⟨⟨ ⟵

Twilight Light

Some babies prefer a night-light to sleep with. Try one that
lights up the ceiling with gentle shining stars.
(My favorite: Twilight Turtle Night Light at www.babybasket.com)

⟶ ⟩⟩ ● ⟨⟨ ⟵

SLEEP CDs

Choose from a variety of CDs that are designed to help baby get to sleep.

My favorites:

Baby Sleep Sweet by Verne Langdon

Classical Lullabies by Big Blue Dog

Lullabies: A Songbook Companion by Essay

Soothing Sounds for Sleep by Hush Little Baby

Magical Lullabies by Big Blue Dog

Sleep My Baby Sleep by Harmonic Convergence

Dreamscape: Lullabies from around the World by Jonathan Elliott, et al.

Sing-A-Long Lullabies by SRT Music

Sleep Baby Sleep by Nicolette Larson

Baby Sleep by Thomas Hampson, et al.

The Planet Sleeps by Sony

BEDTIME BOOKS

Collect and read nursery rhymes and picture books that offer stories about getting ready for bed, bedtime routines, and going to sleep.

My favorites:

Goodnight Moon by Margaret Wise Brown

Goodnight, Gorilla by Peggy Rathman

Hush Little Baby by Sylvia Long

Sleepy Bears by Mem Fox and Kerry Argent

Time for Bed by Mem Fox and Jan Dyer

Say Goodnight by Helen Oxenbury

Bear Snores On by Karma Wilson

Goodnight Max by Rosemary Wells

Goodnight Spot by Eric Hill

A Child's Goodnight Book by Margaret Wise Brown

A Kiss Goodnight by Amy Hest

Nasal Aspirator

If your baby has a stuffy nose, it may be keeping her awake at night.
Use a nasal aspirator to clear the nasal passages and help baby breathe better.
(My favorite: Nasal Aspirator at www.baby-wise.com)

Rocking Feet

These specially created pads attach to the bottom of your
baby's crib and rock him to sleep.
(My favorite: Lullabubs at www.boingboing.net)

Room Fan

Turn on a room fan to help the air circulate and to make white
noise to lull the baby to sleep. Even better, buy one that fits in
with your baby's room decor or theme and is interesting to look at.
(My favorite: www.noblewinds.com)

Mommy Doll

Since Baby attaches to her mother's scent, you might want
to invest in a doll that absorbs your smell while you hold it,
then gives off your scent when you offer it to baby. You can
create your own by holding the doll close to you for a while.
(My favorite: the Waldorf Towel Doll at www.thebabylane.com)

Car-Seat Pillows

If your baby falls asleep in the car seat but looks uncomfortable,
buy a car-seat pillow that provides support for his head.
(My favorites: www.kidalog.net and www.babyage.com)

Chapter 9

Sweet Sounds:
Lullabies and Nursery Rhymes

○ ◗ ● ◖ ○

Lullabies are parents' universal language when it comes to getting baby to sleep. There's nothing like a sweet song to soothe your baby to sleep. Much like white noise, gentle lyrics relax your baby and hypnotize him into drifting off. You don't even have to stay on key as long as you choose simple lullabies and sing them softly. Here are some of my favorite bedtime lullabies and nursery rhymes to help lull your baby to sleep.

KEY NOTES WHEN SINGING TO YOUR BABY

- Sing softly.

- Choose slow songs rather than up-tempo tunes.

- Try to maintain the same rhythm, tone, and volume throughout to help hypnotize your baby to sleep.

- Repeat the song over and over. Babies love repetition.

- Make up new verses if you forget the lines or get tired of the old ones.

- Add your baby's name or other familiar names to the song.

Hush, Little Baby

Hush, little baby, don't say a word.
Papa's gonna buy you a mockingbird.
And if that mockingbird won't sing,
Papa's gonna buy you a diamond ring.
And if that diamond ring turns brass,
Papa's gonna buy you a looking glass.
And if that looking glass gets broke,
Papa's gonna buy you a billy goat.
And if that billy goat won't pull,

Papa's gonna buy you a cart and bull.
And if that cart and bull fall down,
You'll still be the sweetest little baby in town.

Twinkle, Twinkle, Little Star

Twinkle, twinkle, little star
How I wonder what you are!
Up above the world so high
Like a diamond in the sky.
Twinkle, twinkle, little star
How I wonder what you are.

Itsy-Bitsy Spider

The itsy-bitsy spider
Climbed up the waterspout.
Down came the rain
And washed the spider out.
Out came the sun
And dried up all the rain
And the itsy-bitsy spider
Climbed up the spout again.

'Brahms' Lullaby (Lullaby and Good Night)

Lullaby and good night, with roses bedight
With lilies o'er spread is baby's wee bed.
Lay thee down now and rest, may thy slumber
       be blessed.
Lay thee down now and rest, may thy slumber
       be blessed.
Lullaby and good night, thy mother's delight.
Bright angels beside my darling abide.
They will guard thee at rest, thou shalt wake
       on my breast.
They will guard thee at rest, thou shalt wake
       on my breast.

You Are My Sunshine

The other night, dear, as I lay sleeping
I dreamed I held you in my arms.
But when I awoke, dear, I was mistaken,
So I hung my head and I cried.

You are my sunshine, my only sunshine.
You make me happy when skies are gray.
You'll never know, dear, how much I love you.
Please don't take my sunshine away.

Frère Jacques (Are You Sleeping?)

Frère Jacques, Frère Jacques,
Dormez-vous? Dormez-vous?
Sonnez les matines, sonnez les matines,
Ding ding dong, ding ding dong.

(English version)
Are you sleeping, are you sleeping,
Brother John, Brother John?
Morning bells are ringing, morning bells are ringing,
Ding ding dong, ding ding dong.

Baa, Baa, Black Sheep

Baa, baa, black sheep,
Have you any wool?
Yes, sir, yes, sir,
Three bags full.
One for the master,
One for the dame,
And one for the little boy
Who lives down the lane.
Baa, baa, black sheep,
Have you any wool?
Yes, sir, yes, sir,
Three bags full.

One to mend the jerseys,
one to mend the socks,
and one to mend the holes in
the little girls' frocks.
Baa, baa, black sheep,
Have you any wool?
Yes, sir, yes, sir,
Three bags full.

It's Raining, It's Pouring

It's raining, it's pouring;
The old man is snoring.
He went to bed
And he bumped his head,
And he couldn't get up in the morning.

Rock-A-Bye Baby

Rock-a-bye baby, in the treetop.
When the wind blows, the cradle will rock.
When the bough breaks, the cradle will fall,
And down will come baby, cradle, and all.

Mother Goose Rhymes and Poems—
Talk Your Baby To Sleep

You don't have sing to your baby to get her to sleep. Sometimes just the sound of your voice, soft and monotone, will do the trick. Here are some simple and familiar rhymes you can read to your baby or memorize and recite at bedtime.

Sleep, Baby, Sleep

Sleep, baby, sleep
Our cottage vale is deep:
The little lamb is on the green,
With woolly fleece so soft and clean—
Sleep, baby, sleep.
Sleep, baby, sleep,
Down where the woodbines creep;
Be always like the lamb so mild,
A kind, and sweet, and gentle child.
Sleep, baby, sleep.

Bedtime

The Man in the Moon looked out of the moon,
Looked out of the moon and said,
"'Tis time for all children on the earth
To think about getting to bed!"

Bye, Baby Bunting

Bye, baby bunting,
Father's gone a-hunting,
Mother's gone a-milking,
Sister's gone a-silking,
And Brother's gone to buy a skin
To wrap the baby bunting in.

Come, Let's To Bed

"To bed! To bed!"
Says Sleepy-head;
"Tarry awhile," says Slow;
"Put on the pan,"
Says Greedy Nan,
"We'll sup before we go."

Hush-A-Bye

Hush-a-bye, baby, lie still with thy daddy.
Thy mammy has gone to the mill,
To get some meal to bake a cake,
So pray, my dear baby, lie still.

Hush-a-bye, baby,
Daddy is near;
Mamma is a lady,
And that's very clear.

Hush Baby Dolly

Hush, baby, my dolly, I pray you don't cry,
And I'll give you some bread, and some
      milk by-and-by;
Or perhaps you like custard, or maybe a tart,
Then to either you're welcome, with all of
      my heart.

Resources

Products

Here are some of the best places to find baby sleep aids.

AROMATHERAPY DOLLS: www.babysenchantedgarden.com,
www.blueherondolls.com

BABY SLEEP POSITIONER: www.mypreciousbaby.com,
www.sleepwellbaby.com, www.netkidswear.com

BODY PILLOW: www.babyemporio.com, www.babysleepwell.com,
www.babycenter.com

CAR-SEAT SUPPORT: www.mypreciousbaby.com, www.babycenter.com

COLIC SOOTHER: www.kidatheartdesigns.com, www.colic.com,
www.parenting.com

COMFORTER: www.babysleepshop.com, www.babybox.com,
www.babyuniverse.com

CO-SLEEPING PRODUCTS: www.nurturecenter.com,
www.armsreach.com, www.betterforbabies.com

HEARTBEAT SOUNDS: www.babygotosleep.com, www.geniusbabies.com,
www.babysleepsystem.com, www.slumbersounds.com

MASSAGE OILS AND KITS:
www.slumbersounds.com, www.babymassage.net, www.natureschild.com

MOTION BEDS:
www.floatingbed.com, www.babyage.com, www.babyuniverse.com,
www.ambybaby.com

SIMULATED SUNRISE-AND-SUNSET MACHINE: www.sleepwellbaby.com, www.sunshinesales.ca

SLEEP CDS: www.slumbersounds.com, www.hush-baby.com

SLEEPING BAG: www.babysleepshop.com, www.baby-sleeping-bags.com, www.sleephuggers.com, www.babyinabag.com

SLEEP-SOUND GENERATOR: www.babysleeptraining.com, www.sleepwellbaby.com, www.naturestapestry.com, www.sleeptightinfantsoother.com

SLEEP WEDGES AND FORMS: www.securebaby.com, www.mypreciouskid.com, www.netkidswear.com

SLUMBER BEAR: www.sleepsounds.com, www.babysleepshop.com, www.securebaby.com

SOUNDS OF THE WOMB: www.babysleepsystem.com, www.ciaobellababy.com, www.happymothers.com

SWADDLERS: www.mypreciousbaby.com, www.babyuniverse.com, www.swaddledesigns.com, www.pregnancystore.com, www.babysupermall.com

WHITE-NOISE MACHINE: www.sleepwellbaby.com, www.cdbaby.com, www.purewhitenoise.com

Reading

If you want more help on almost any topic related to parenting, check out these resourceful sites for tips and discussions on all aspects of baby care.

www.americanbaby.com

www.baby.com

www.babycenter.com

www.baby-parenting.com

www.babysleeptraining.com

www.babyzone.com

www.cozybabies.com

www.familyresource.com

www.ivillage.com

www.parent.com

www.pregnancyandbaby.com

www.pregnancyandbirth.com

www.sleepingbabyheaven.com

www.sleepwellbaby.com

www.talkaboutsleep.com

Acknowledgments

Many thanks to the parents and professionals who offered their best advice for getting back to sleep: Kay Ambrose, Vidhya Balaji, Lucy Balyan, Sansa Brien, Trudy Cain, Norma Carlson, Ray Cipolla, Isobel Cope, Laura Coughlin, Lima Cranford, JoAnne Dahlin, Shirley Davis, Bonnie DeCosta, Mohina Devi, Lisa Duran, Karen Dyer, Linda Edman, Brie Fairbanks, Tracy Fontecilla, Bernadette Galang, Elizabeth Gentry, Kelly Genzlinger, Anne Gilbertson, Rachel Goetting, Barbara Grant, Patricia Grant, Claudia Guerra, Vicki Huynh, Julaina Kliest, Holly Kralj, Jean Krumboltz, Rena Leith, Mary Libbey, Kristin Littlefield, Cindy Ma, Amy McCurdy, Susan McGrath, Staci McLaughlin, Michael Melvin, Rebecca Melvin, Shauna Melvin, Dana Mentink, Sheila Merghati, Deanna Mitchell, Rachel Montemayor, Stefany Moreno, Valerie Mozee, Jennifer O'Connor, Kathleen O'Leary, Arianna Orleans, Ann Parker, Connie Pike, Geoffrey Pike, Sally Pioroda, Carole Price, Rafhat Rafiuddin, David Raitz, Courtney Rapa, Dina Rosin, Chris Saunders, Chell Schauben, Victoria Stadelhofer, Barbara Swec, Amy Szucs, Catie Thiebaud, Heather Thornton, Camille Thompson, Janet Tilander, Cynthia Tinsley, Timmy Tran, Amritha Umesh, Susan Warner, Candi Wensley, Cyrena Wood, Julie Zhu, and several more who prefer to remain anonymous.

Very special thanks to my amazing agents, Lilly Ghahremani and Stefanie Von Borstel, and my wonderful editor, Kate Prouty.

Index